BASIC VOLLEYBALL STRATEGY

RICHARD B. LYTTLE

Basic Volleyball Strategy

An Introduction
for Young Players

*Illustrated with diagrams
by John Lane*

DOUBLEDAY & COMPANY, INC.   GARDEN CITY, NEW YORK

ISBN 0-385-14062-2 Trade
    0-385-14063-0 Prebound

Library of Congress Catalog Card Number 78–1210

This book is for
Howard Brose

Contents

Preface

This book assumes that you know the rules and understand that their primary purpose is to preserve the speed and clean excitement of the game of volleyball, a game that is won on individual talent and highly polished teamwork. Every player should have access to the United States Volleyball Association Rule Book. If you don't have one handy, you or someone on your team should request one by writing the association at P. O. Box 77065, San Francisco, CA 94107. Enclose $2.35 for purchase and postage.

At first glance, the rule book may look technical and complex, but it is surprising how a quick reference to it will silence debate or clear up any points that may be cloudy in your own mind. Obviously, you must follow the rules to the letter if you are to become a valuable player.

One other obvious point. Play with the proper equipment. You will never improve your game by passing a beach ball around or spiking over a sagging net. Pay particular attention to the net. No matter if it is seven feet high for junior high play, seven, four-and-a-quarter for the women's game, or eight feet for the men's game, it must be tight top and bottom.

Now, let's begin.

BASIC VOLLEYBALL STRATEGY

Offensive Strategy

1

THE SERVE

Variety: The server who brings several different serves into the game will always be a big asset to his or her team. And on the other side of the coin, the server who dishes up the same ball from the back corner time after time will be a serious handicap. Even if you have perfected one type of serve, it will not be very effective when your opponents always know it's coming.

Many beginning players have the idea that there are just two types of serves in volleyball—the floater and the spinner. This notion ignores all the subtle variations that top-notch players have mastered, the variations that keep the opposition guessing, that sometimes win points

3

outright, and that often force the other team to start its offense with a desperation play.

The best players always include serving practice in their workouts to maintain a large arsenal of accurate serves.

Underhand: For beginners, the underhand serve is the easiest to control. It allows inexperienced players to get into a game with very little preparation and benefit from the exercise and fun of volleyball.

The underhand serve

Face the net with a well-balanced stance, knees slightly bent. For right-handers, the left foot should be advanced, closer to the service line than the right foot. (Left-handers in following instructions throughout this book must reverse sides. In this case, the right foot would be advanced for a left-handed server.)

Hold the ball on the palm of your lead hand, the left for right-handers. Swing your hitting arm back, elbow straight but not locked. As you swing your arm back, your weight should shift to the back foot. Then, as the arm moves forward, your weight should shift forward to the front foot. Bring the arm forward briskly to hit the ball either with the heel of your hand or the knuckle face and heel of your fist. Some servers toss the ball slightly with their holding hand just before impact. Others simply let the holding hand drop away as the strike is made. In either case, avoid putting a spin on the ball with your release.

The underhand toss serve

By limiting your follow-through, you make the ball float over the net with no spin. The floating ball dips and dances in flight because the impact has distorted its spherical shape. As it adjusts from impact, the ball presents changing surfaces to wind resistance. This makes it act like a knuckle-ball pitch, and it keeps the receiver guessing.

5

Had the serve come off your hand spinning, the effect of ball distortion would have been canceled, and the ball's path would have been predictable. Spin is desirable on many hard serves, but rarely is it an advantage when serving underhand. This serve is slow, and unless you have some unusual technique, you must count on a floating ball for deception.

The action of a floating ball can be somewhat controlled by valve-seat position. Remember, the ball is light, between 250 and 280 grams, and has a diameter of twenty-five to twenty-seven inches. This means that the weight of the valve seat affects wind resistance and ball action. Experiment with different positions. You will find that serving with the valve seat up will usually cause the ball to take a sudden drop soon after crossing the net. Serving with the valve seat toward the net will produce more side-to-side action. By changing positions of the valve seat during your turn at the service line, you can bring that all-important variety into your serves.

Overhand: Some good servers will occasionally use the underhand serve as a surprise tactic, but more than 99 per cent of the serves in serious competition are hit overhand. These serves have much more speed and a shorter trajectory than the underhand, and once you have mastered the technique, you will have more accuracy serving overhand. Veteran player and coach Gene Selznick says the difference between underhand and overhand serving is like the difference between playing softball or hardball on the baseball diamond.

Power for the overhand serve comes from full body motion and a forward stride into the hit. This means that you must start three or four feet behind the service line to avoid a foul. Like a serve in tennis, the timing for an overhand serve is vital. And like a tennis serve, there are many different but effective styles. Keep in mind that results are more important than style, and don't be afraid to experiment to find out what style works best for you.

Right-handers should start with the left foot forward, knees slightly bent, and slightly more weight on the back foot. Start with the ball about waist high, the tossing hand under the ball and the hitting hand on top. The toss is vital for good delivery. The peak of the toss should be about three feet above your head, and just enough in front of you so that you can keep your eyes glued to the ball without strain or loss of balance. Follow the ball up with the tossing hand and bring the hitting hand back behind your ear by cocking your elbow. The elbow should be about neck high, pointed away from the body. At this point, bring your tossing hand down as you stride forward. Extend your hitting arm fully and hit the ball squarely. Impact and follow-through depend on the kind of serve you wish to deliver.

The Flat Serve: Like the floating underhand serve, the flat overhand serve will dip, bob, and weave. Impact can be made with a closed fist, but more deception can be achieved by keeping the hand open and making impact with the heel of the hand only.

7

The overhand flat serve

Follow-through must be limited. If you bring the hand down with too much force on the follow-through, the ball will spin, and you will not get the desired knuckle-ball effect of a flat serve. If your ball spins, try freezing after impact with your hitting arm pointing after the ball. If this does not cure the problem, it may be that you are putting too much hand on the ball. Cock your wrist back to keep palm and fingers off the ball.

Because this serve is much harder than the underhand floater, valve-seat position has greater influence on ball action.

8

The Top-spin Serve: The receiver should not be able to tell the difference between this serve and the flat serve until after you have hit the ball. This is why a flat serve with a closed fist is not recommended. Very few servers can spin a ball effectively off a closed fist.

The overhand top-spin serve

Use the stance and motions of the overhand flat serve. The main difference will be in the impact and follow-through. The heel of your hand must hit the ball slightly off center and your fingers must make contact on the follow-through to add to the spinning motion. Your hitting arm will come down across your body just as it does when you throw a baseball overhand. The arm follow-through should be the first warning that the receiver has to get ready for a spinning serve.

The top spin should be fast and it should angle down abruptly soon after crossing the net. Combined with the

9

flat serve, the top spin will give a change of pace that will prevent receivers from digging in against you. The top spin, however, is a difficult serve to master. It takes hours of practice to learn what point of impact and follow-through will work best for you. But the time you spend on this serve will pay off, and the top spin offers opportunity for innovation. By varying point of impact and putting wrist turn into your hit, you might be able to hit a highly deceptive curve. Nothing demoralizes a receiver and his teammates as much as an "out" serve that curves back, untouched to hit inside the line for an easy point.

The Roundhouse Serve: The Japanese developed this style to add more speed to the flat serve. It works for the Japanese, but the technique seems to lose something in translation for most American players. You, however, may be an exception. If it works for you, the roundhouse will be one more weapon in your arsenal.

Stand with left side toward the net. Your right arm, fully extended, is brought back and down as you start the toss with your left hand. Weight will shift back to the right foot. As you swing your hitting arm up to meet the ball, you should lift your left foot to stride forward, shifting your weight to that foot at the point of impact. As with the flat overhand serve, you must restrict follow-through to avoid spin. With so much body motion going into the serve, it is very difficult for some servers to limit follow-through. Also, you may have difficulty keeping this ball in your opponent's court. If you tend to overhit, you will have to stand farther back from the service line. This means the ball will stay in the air longer than an

The overhand roundhouse serve

overhead serve, giving the opponents more time to get set.

Advantages of the roundhouse are debatable. It looks intimidating, and it is a faster ball when hit properly, but it is hard to match the accuracy of the overhead serve—spin or flat.

The Sidearm Serve: It is almost impossible to aim this serve effectively. It is similar to an underhand serve, except the ball is hit to the side rather than the front of the body. It is mentioned here only to encourage experimentation. It just might work for you. If it doesn't, forget it. You will be better off using the underhand serve until you have mastered the overhand technique.

Tips

1. Serving out means a side out and a loss of scoring opportunity. Accuracy is a must. Even an easy serve puts the ball in play and gives your team a chance.

2. In serious competition, no single serve, no matter how polished, will give you an offensive edge. Work for variety, the greater the better.

3. Experiment with all kinds of serves, keep searching for the style that fits your ability.

4. Don't neglect serving in practice sessions and pre-game warm-ups. Constant attention is needed for pinpoint timing.

5. Deception is an important facet of serving. Don't telegraph your serve by changing stance or delivery. Keep your opponents guessing.

2

THE PASS

The Pivot Play: How you receive a serve determines how well your team makes the transition from defense to offense. In fact, the pass can be described as both a defensive and an offensive maneuver. If you learn to make the play properly, even on the toughest serves, you will be a solid asset to any team.

⤫ *The Bump Pass:* Move to a position in front of the ball so that the mid-line of your body is lined up with the ball's path. You have to be light on your feet, ready to slide or hop to maintain alignment as the ball approaches. Getting set too soon can leave you reaching awkwardly for a lively ball.

The bump pass

Keep your hands in front of you as you lean forward, watching the ball. This gives you a balanced stance that will allow those last-minute adjustments. You want the ball to arrive about waist high, and you adjust body level mostly with a knee bend. Passers usually stand in a modified crouch, feet well apart with one foot ahead of the other, and arms about eighteen inches in front of the hips.

Before the ball arrives, bring your hands together

14

making a pad for the bump with your forearms just above the wrists. There are two ways to link your hands to assure a level pad, one that does not cause a double-

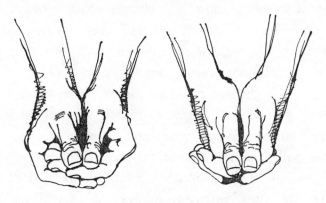

The two-hand positions for the bump pass

hit foul or a deflected pass. One method calls for interlocked fingers with the thumbs at the top, side by side. The other method calls for cupping the fingers of one hand inside the palm of the other, again with thumbs parallel on top.

Some passers rotate their arms outward to expose a flatter area of the forearm by separating the thumbs. The thumbs remain parallel with the palms of the cupped hands facing almost straight up.

Try tossing the ball and bumping it with your forearms several times to find your most comfortable hand position. Remember that your hands must be together and on the same level. This puts your forearms in solid position for the pass, and it allows you to get a reasonably good hit off your thumbs if you should misjudge the

15

ball. If your hands separate at any time during contact, you will be called for a double-hit foul.

When the ball hits, keep your arms rigid. Any lift you give to the rebounding ball should come mostly from knee flex. This produces a soft pass that you can control and that your setter, the next player in the offensive pattern, can handle with confidence.

If the ball flutters or curves away from your body mid-line at the last minute, giving you no time to change your stance, you will have to reach to one side for the ball. You must twist your entire body with the reach, making sure your arms retain their level hitting surface. Reaching with arm motion alone will produce an errant pass or an out-of-bounds ball.

Reaching may influence your choice of hand grip. Some passers, for instance, find that body twist comes more easily when they use an interlocking grip. Others are more comfortable with the cupped grip.

In the heat of a rally, you will have to reach, dig, and dive to get off your pass, but if you are forced to make desperation plays time after time on receiving serve, you and your teammates should check position. Normally, front-line players should station themselves near the center of the court, letting balls at waist level or higher go by for the back-court receivers. Back-court players should stand near the end line where they have full view of the serve and can run forward into the pass at any angle. Take a back-court position that allows you to let waist-high serves go by, knowing they will fall out of bounds.

The one-handed bump pass

Usually the serve will be hard enough to rebound off your stiff forearms with its own momentum, but you must be ready to spring your elbows for that soft serve which needs a boost. Keep your arms relaxed until the moment of contact. Then snap your elbows into the locked position and put enough force behind the ball to deliver it to your target. This takes precision timing, and that means practice.

You must also practice the bump pass in a low crouch and on your knees so that you can handle fast-dropping top-spin serves. It takes much more arm action to get off a pass when your knees are deeply bent or on the floor.

The Overhand Pass: In the early days of volleyball, passes were made with spread hands just above the up-turned face. The receiver watched the ball into the hands and shoved it off to the target. This pass is perfectly legal. It is the standard method for setting a ball, but it is rarely used by serve receivers today mainly because of the trouble it gives referees. Off a hard serve, it is

↘ The overhand pass

difficult to determine if the overhead receiver touched simultaneously with both hands or made an illegal double hit. The bump pass makes play move faster by keeping referees' calls to a minimum.

The overhead pass will be discussed at length in the next chapter. For now, just remember that it is a technique you can use if you cannot get into a good position to make a bump pass.

Saves: There will be times when all you can do with a serve is keep it from hitting the floor, trying in a desperation play to get it up high enough for a teammate to handle. Against good servers, such plays can be all too common. You must learn to make a one armed pass off your wrist, using a stiff arm for power and accuracy.

You should also master the backward pass, taking the ball over your head and bumping it back to a teammate. When you can make good desperation passes that give your setter a reasonably good ball time after time, you will take the edge away from those hot servers on the other side of the net. Passers who can put the ball up perfectly from a dive or a dig are thrilling to watch, particularly when they are on your side.

Placement: Where and how you pass the ball will be determined largely by your team's offensive tactics. In all serious play, you will have a designated setter, and you must learn how he or she likes the ball.

When there are right-hand hitters on the line, the setter will probably stand slightly to the right and face the hitter on the left—the on-side hitter, that is, the one who will receive the ball on his or her hitting hand side.

High-lob passes are easiest for setters to handle. Inexperienced teams use the high lob almost exclusively, but as you and your teammates improve, you should use low passes that move quickly to the net, giving the opposition little time to prepare a defense. Low, accurate passing is the trademark of a top-notch team.

Tips

1. Passing is the pivot play of the game. A well-made pass is an offensive play. A poor one will not get your offense started.

2. A player who cannot execute an accurate bump pass from all angles of approach will be the weak link on a team. The opposing server will always try to put the ball in his or her area of the court.

3. Develop a clean style that will not attract attention from the referee. If your hands separate at impact or if your forearms don't form a level pad for the ball you will be called for a double hit.

4. Find out what kind of passes your setter likes. The setter has the most difficult job in the offensive pattern, don't make it any tougher with a poor pass.

5. If you and your teammates have continued trouble receiving serves, you may not be in good position. Adjust your court coverage to pick up the problem areas.

3

THE SET

The Quarterback: Like a football quarterback, the setter in volleyball receives most of the criticism when the offense breaks down, but when the offense works, the volleyball setter rarely gets the credit he or she deserves. Those high jumping, hard-hitting strikers take the glory.

Actually, any veteran of serious competition, particularly premium hitters, will tell you that good setting is the key to any offense, and that a player who can do the job properly play after play is hard to find. The ideal setter would combine intelligence with a distinctive feel for the game. Anticipation, speed, lightning reflexes, and peripheral vision would also be handy. Few athletes come close to the ideal, and this is why competitive teams operate with designated setters. These teams want the best players available to take responsibility for the set.

Setters must know all aspects of the game. They must read the opposition's defensive patterns and anticipate movement of the blockers. Setters must be aware of the strength and weaknesses of their own teammates, particularly the hitters. They must know how to create the scoring opportunities by playing to strength. And, of course, they must have the skill to accomplish all this.

There are basically six different kinds of sets, and with up to three hitters on the forward line as targets, the setter has many options to choose from when he or she runs up to take the pass.

Front Set: A well-directed overhand pass describes most set shots, but this makes it sound too easy. You must have educated hands and you must use your entire body to receive the pass and get the ball away with precision.

Start with arms and knees bent. Lift your spread hands about ten inches above your face, making a "window" between the thumb and forefingers of each hand. Watch the ball into your hands through this window. Contact is made with the pads of the fingers in a cushioning action with knees and elbows bending to soften contact. Hands should rotate inward as the ball is received and outward with the push off. Sight your target over the top of the ball and send it off with minimum spin.

The front set

Feet should remain on the ground, spread enough for a well-balanced base, up to the point when you flex your knees in a jumping action that will lift you to your toes and perhaps off the floor as you send the ball on its way. Straightened elbows give further boost to the ball.

A good setter will cushion the ball for a long time without being called for a held-ball foul. Watching the action is something like watching a slow-motion film.

Setting is similar to a swing in golf. There is so much for a beginner to think about that conscious effort sometimes spoils the action. You must practice until your moves become subconscious, freeing your mind to concentrate on placement and trajectory.

For most front sets, you will give the ball a high trajectory so that your spiker can time the approach and leap to the ball. Your position will be two or three feet from the net with one side toward the net. The ball you set will travel parallel to the net.

Your position gives you a chance for deception with a different play.

Back Set: This involves the same motions as the front set until you make contact. At that point you must arch

The back set

your back and guide the ball over your head to a target behind you. Your feet will not leave the ground, and it is not likely that you will get as much distance as you do with your front set.

The main value of this play is deception. When blockers anticipate a spike off a front set and begin moving too soon, you must be ready to play the back set. If you give away your intentions with a backward glance or early arching of the back, you will lose the advantage of the play.

Side Set: When the setter receives the ball with his or her back to the net, it is possible to direct it to either

The side, or lateral, set

side at the last minute without giving the opposition any clue to which way it is going. It is necessary, however, to cushion the ball even longer for this maneuver, and referees, particularly those locked in on the traditional front- and back-set methods, may call fouls every time they see a side set.

Another disadvantage is that the setter does not have the benefit of seeing the defensive alignment of the team across the net. And it must be said that side-setting calls for sophisticated ball handling, usually beyond the capabilities of beginning and intermediate players.

Jump: There will sometimes be high passes that you cannot reach without jumping. When these come to you above the net, you are presented with an offensive option you must turn to advantage. The other team has no way of knowing if you will spike the ball yourself or set it for a teammate. What you do depends on the defense across the net. As you jump in the air, you must use your peripheral vision to check the defenders.

If blockers have committed themselves, set to a teammate. If you have a clear shot, spike the ball.

For setting in the air, use the standard form, making a window with your hands and guiding the ball with your fingers and arm thrust. Timing will differ with just about every jump-set situation, and you can achieve perfection only through practice. Good setters always make the best of bad passes, and bad passes occur even on the best teams.

Low Set: Low passes are tougher to handle than high ones. You may have to drop to your knees, sit, or even roll to your back to get under the ball. Without the flex of your legs, you must use stronger arm and wrist action to get the ball up for the spikers. Again, it takes practice to handle the low pass and keep your team's offense alive.

In the heat of a game, it is often tempting to blame your problems on the passer when the truth of the matter is that both of you need more practice.

Short Set: This important offensive weapon takes good teamwork and a setter with a fine touch. Most sets have a high trajectory which gives your spiker time to run, jump, and hit. With the short set, the ball is put up just one or two feet above the net with a soft touch. Your spiker must start running while you take the pass, so you must put the ball in just the right spot for his or her hit. This is sometimes called the one set or the two set, depending on the distance in feet that the ball is placed above the net.

The short set can catch a defense off balance, particularly if blockers have been conditioned for high sets and are not prepared for the fast-breaking play. It also opens up an excellent fake. Your spiker can start the run as if a short set is coming. This will draw the blockers to that side of the net while you set to the other side, giving a teammate there a big opening for the spike.

Footwork: Setters have other duties. Some strategic patterns call for the setter to rush to the net from the back court, take the pass, then back up the hitter to protect against blocked ball, and, finally, run back to cover a position in the back court on defense. You must be fast on your feet to play this kind of volleyball.

Other strategic patterns are not so demanding, but you must still use fast footwork to be in the right position during all phases of the game. In fast play, the ball may change sides every two seconds. This does not give you much time to think about where you should be. Your footwork must be instinctive. Move on the balls of your feet, ready to change direction, jump, or dive in an instant.

Tips

1. Good setting is the key to offense.
2. You must have the ability to set the ball up where you want it off the bad passes as well as the good ones.
3. Practice setting until you make the play instinctively without the conscious thoughts that might distract you.
4. A setter who can make all sets well—front, back, high, low, and short—will keep the defense guessing. Side sets can add to your versatility, and some players use the move almost exclusively with good results.

5. The setter is the busiest player on the court, moving up for the pass and running back to defend. Develop fast footwork.

6. Know where your spikers like the ball; recognize your team's patterns; be alert for change in tempo; read the defensive alignment across the net; be the quarterback.

4

THE SPIKE

The Basics: A high jump and a powerful hit are important in spiking, but you cannot achieve either of these goals until after you have mastered the basics. In fact, hard hitting and a high jump without the basics will not win points.

The basics are approach, timing, and aim. When you have mastered these, you will be able to make volleyball's most dramatic play. And your jumping ability will increase as you continue your play and your workouts.

The Approach: Three strides at least are needed for players with average jumping ability. If you are right-handed, you probably will step out with the left foot,

The spike

then the right as you build up speed to plant the left foot again and jump. Style, however, varies with individuals—you may be more comfortable beginning with your right foot, and you may also find that it takes you more than three steps to build up momentum.

It is usually best to jump with both feet. This helps control your lift so that you go straight up and avoid a net-touch foul.

In almost all cases you should approach at an angle. This also helps keep you off the net, and the angle gives you the best sight on the ball and best peripheral view of the defensive set up. It also allows adjustments as you step up for the jump without having to lunge to one side or the other and risk losing your balance.

As you practice your approach, think of the first step as the one that directs you toward your jumping spot, the second that lines your body up behind the ball, and the third the power step that gives you your lift. During the approach, the arms should be at your sides to assure good balance. On your jump step, swing the arms back, extending them behind you. Then as your knees flex for the lift, bring both arms up vigorously, letting them reach into the air and give momentum to your lift. Your hitting arm will naturally carry back, elbow cocked with the hand behind your ear.

Timing: Begin your approach about seven feet from the net, and if you are spiking from a corner, stay close to the side line to make sure you keep the ball in the court. Make sure also that the ball is set before you begin your run. A short set, of course, calls for an earlier start, but you will not be ready for this play until you learn to spike high sets effectively.

Beginners often start running too early. They peak while the ball is still out of reach above their heads. For power and control you must peak in position to hit down on the ball, and you must be behind the ball, not under it.

As you start your jump with full knee flex, arch your back to put more power in your hit. No matter what style you develop, try to use the same jump for all hits. Dink shots will not be effective if you telegraph your intentions by some change in your approach, jump, or arm position.

Practice your approach and jump without the ball to find your best style. You should land on or close to your take-off spot. When you can jump well consistently, have a friend set balls for you so you can work on your timing. Of course, you will also begin working on your hit.

A hard spike is hit in much the same way you hit a top-spin serve except that you will be hitting down on the ball. The heel of the hand carries into the ball, your wrist should snap forward, bringing the extended fingers onto the ball to give spin and extra power for your spike.

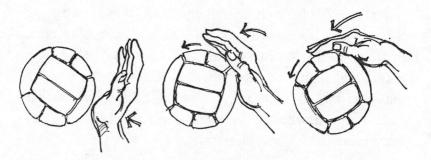

How wrist snap gives spiked ball spin.

Follow-through should be in the direction of the hit, but it has to be restricted to avoid a net touch. You can follow-through over the net provided ball contact was on your side, but you must draw the hand back quickly to avoid a touch on the way down.

Work on hits from all positions at the net, but concentrate on the corners where most of the sets will be made and where you will have the best scoring opportunities.

Aim: The blocker who moves directly in front of you on a corner shot will often open up a lane down the alley for a good spike. If the middle blocker comes up to join an end blocker, the end man may "cheat" too much toward the line, giving you an opening between the two players. If the middle blocker tries to close this gap, you can hit a cross-court spike.

If the blocking is faultless, you might be able to score by dinking over the block, or hitting a carom shot off the end blocker's arm for an out of bounds point. Carom shots don't have much chance from the middle of the net. Also, you are likely to face three blockers on those mid-court shots.

You will have best power and control from sets that come to you on your hitting arm side. This is called an on-hand spike. You will not have quite as much power and control when you must reach across your body to hit a set coming from the other side, an off-hand spike.

Don't try to be a switch-hitter. That might work in baseball, but ambidextrous spikers in volleyball are practically nonexistent. If you are naturally right-handed, hit with your right hand. If you are a southpaw, hit with your left. Trying to hit with either hand is liable to turn you into a poor hitter with both hands. Instead, you should strive for equal accuracy with both on-hand and off-hand shots.

Your strongest shots will most likely be on balls hit down and away from you on an on-hand set. Thus, a right-hander hitting from the left corner of the net will get most power on the shot angled to the opposite side

Top: The on-hand spike

Bottom: The off-hand spike

of the opponent's court. But good blocking may close off this angle. So the spiker must be able to hit between the blockers at a less acute angle or down the side line if that avenue should be open.

From the right corner of the net, a right-hander taking off-hand sets must look for the same options, an angle cross-court spike, a spike between blockers, and a shot down the line.

Hitting from the middle, the best shot for a right-handed hitter will usually be one that angles right, past the middle blocker, but this has to be done quickly before the end blockers can come in to form a line of defense. This is where short sets less than three feet above the net can be very effective. Equally effective and certainly more spectacular, is a jump set with the setter and the spiker going up together. The spiker hits the ball out of the setter's hands. This, however, is an extremely difficult play to time and is not recommended for beginners.

What you must concentrate on from the very first is accuracy. Power hitters who cannot shoot into the open spaces are a blocker's delight.

Young players who have not attained full height usually exaggerate the importance of body height in spiking. Sure, it would be great to stand six-foot, six and swat those spikes off a hop. But height can limit development. Experienced players and coaches will tell you that many tall players never become good jumpers. Since they do not have to put out the effort, they do not develop the devastating jumps and hits that shorter players do.

The dink

So if you are short, don't be discouraged. Jumping ability can be developed through exercise and vigorous play. If you should be tall, however, and can jump well, you will have the advantage of being able to spike over blockers, but don't go to this shot too often. The backcourt players have a clear view of your hit and can't be taken by surprise easily.

The Dink: Every hitter should develop a well-disguised dink shot. It is important that you use the same approach, jump, and arm motion that you use for your hardest shots. The difference is in the hit. Instead of using the heel of the hand with the follow-through wrist snap, you must take the ball on the pads of your fingers. If the fingers are slightly bent, you can boost the ball by straightening them with your hit. Remember, the ball cannot come to rest on your hand. The dink must be a clean hit. Direction is controlled mainly by your point of contact with the ball. Some players dink with a closed fist to avoid being called for a held ball, but you will get a much more accurate shot with your fingers.

The favorite dink shot goes just over the blockers' hands to the floor behind them. However, when the defense has this area covered, you will be better off angling the ball right or left.

The dink is not a substitute for a hard hit. Instead, it is like a change-up in baseball. It keeps the opponents loose, unable to dig in for the fast ball. It helps make the fast ball more effective.

Soft Spikes: The same can be said for spikes not hit with full velocity. You can keep the defense guessing if you can change velocity. A soft spike will fool a defender who has come to expect your hits to bound high off a pass with their own momentum. Some players can dig the hard ball with much more ease than the soft one. So if you can put your soft hits in the open court, you might well force an error.

Tips

1. Concentrate on the basics; the approach, timing, and aim. Jumping height and hitting power will develop with your play and your workouts.

2. Try to use the same approach and jump for all your spikes. Don't telegraph your intentions to the opposition.

3. Learn to read a defense as you make your approach. Always have a target. Never hit blindly.

4. Vary the speed of your hits with soft spikes and dinks.

5. A wrist snap that brings your fingers in contact with the ball will give it downspin and make it drop. Hard spikes with plenty of downspin will almost always stay in the court.

6. Learn to spike on high sets. After you have mastered the basics, your team can take advantage of the trickier plays, the low sets, and the jump sets.

7. Try not to give up on any set, even the poor ones. An easy volley over the net just to keep the game alive will give your opponents a big edge.

5

BASIC ATTACK

Game Flow: It is misleading in volleyball to think that your team goes on offense as soon as the ball comes into your court. A good serve, for instance, can put you on defense and make it tough to launch any offense.

It also must be stated that the ball changes sides so quickly that it is often impossible to say exactly when offensive play ends and defensive play begins. Offensive and defensive plays tend to flow together. When playing offense, you must always have defense in mind. Adjustments in offensive positioning might well be influenced by the need for a tighter team defense.

Thus, while it is necessary in a book of instruction to talk about offense and defense separately, it will seem like a very arbitrary separation to those who know the game.

Serve Placement: In most cases, the deeper you can serve the better. A deep serve forces the back-court opponents to make long passes to the setter at the net, and most passers have more difficulty making their play moving backward than they do moving forward.

Also, on a deep serve, inexperienced passers may hesitate too long if they think the serve might go out.

Serving to the weakest passers is always a good tactic, but generally it is a very poor practice to serve to any of the front-line players. This gives the passer an easy pass to the setter, and it allows the setter to establish a rhythm with the hitter that often leads to a well-timed attack. A high pass near the net also gives the setter the option of spiking.

If the opposition has balanced passing talent, the back corners make the best serving targets. Players there must decide if your ball will stay within both the back line and the side line, and this can often cause hesitation on a close serve. Against most teams, the left corner has the advantage of forcing the defender to pass the ball up and across the court. This makes it tough for a setter to pass backward. The ball will probably go to the left-side spiker, and your blockers will probably have plenty of time to reach their positions.

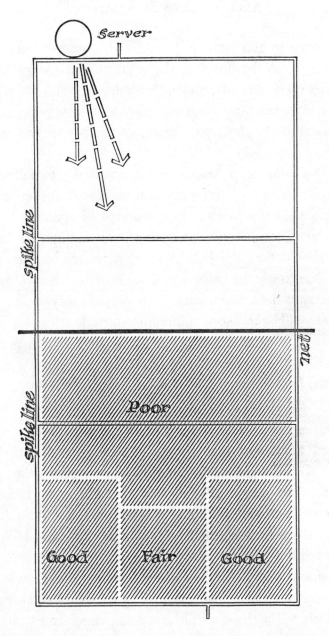

Serve deep to the corners or deep in the center for the best results. A short serve to a poor passer will sometimes win a point,
and you can sometimes use a short serve as a surprise tactic.

A serve to the right corner, on the other hand, may force a set to the hitter at the right side of the net, and this can be an advantage, particularly with a weak, off-hand hitter. Any time you can force your opponents to make your play, you have made a good offensive serve.

Serves sent deep to center are not likely to influence direction of a set, but they can cause confusion when spotted between passers. This works well against players who have not practiced together long enough to know who should take the ball. A short serve made after several long ones can also cause confusion when a front player runs back into a back-court player's way.

You will get more pinpoint control with top-spin serves. As a general rule, your flat floaters should not be aimed for the corners. Just concentrate on putting them into the back court.

Four-spiker Attack: Beginning players, players with limited skill, and teams that lack a good balance of talent should follow the four-spiker, two-setter (the 4-2) system. The alignment calls for two hitters at the net, one near each side line, and a setter in the middle. Two of the three back-court players will be hitters, while the other will be a setter.

Positions should be taken for a rotation that will always put a setter in the front line. In other words, every third player of the six will be a setter. Back-court players can spike if they start their jumps behind the spike line, but such a play is not as effective as spiking at the net. It should be used only when poor passing or setting forces a back-court attack.

When one of the two setters is at the middle of the net when the serve is received, there is no need for a shift. However, if the setter is on one of the side lines, he or she must shift to the middle, changing positions with a hitter as soon as the serve is made. This puts the setter in position to receive the pass.

Forward and back setting give the main variations in the 4-2 system. When the setter can disguise the play so that the defenders can't guess if a forward or back set is coming before the ball is in the air, the spiker can often beat the blockers. It is important for the setter to be able to face either left or right and make forward or back sets with equal ease from either position.

Some additional variation can be developed by changing the depth of a set. Most hitters, however, handle the shallow ball close to the net better than the deeper one four or five feet back. But if you have a good, deep hitter on your team, you can use the variation to advantage.

Short sets, when players have the skill for it, fit in well with the 4-2 system. The set must be perfectly timed and placed, and this is difficult to do if the pass has not been perfect. Since the spiker must start jumping before the short set goes up, you will need a signal system to start the play.

After a short set starts working for you, use the short set fake. When a spiker begins a run to one side of the net, blockers will almost always be drawn to that side,

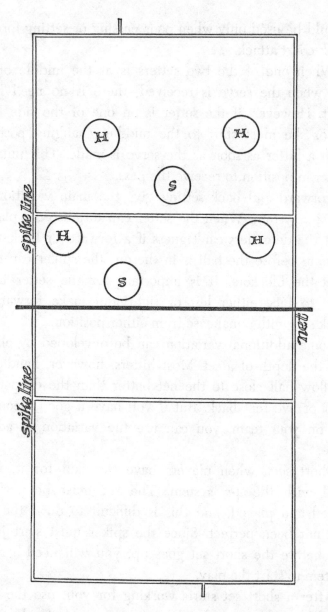

The line-up for the 4-2 offense will always have one of your designated setters in the forward line, ready to move to the net for a
pass, usually from a back-court player.

giving the hitter on the other side an open target. This play also takes perfect placement and timing.

Despite the above variations, the options in a 4-2 system are limited. When you gain enough talent for serious competition you will play the more advanced three-hitter system described in the next chapter.

Tips

1. Serve deep and toward the corners. Try to make the receiver back up and hesitate with the hope of an out call. Force the long pass to the setter.

2. Use a spin serve for shaving the side lines. With floaters, just concentrate on keeping the serve in the back court.

3. Use the four-spiker, two-setter system until your team has mastered all skills of the game. Although the system has limitations, it still produces plenty of exciting play.

4. As with all systems, good setting is vital in the 4-2 attack. Poor back setting or inability to disguise intentions will take the punch out of your offense.

5. Make use of available talent. A tall player who can spike a deep set, a setter and hitter who can combine for the short set will provide important variations.

47

6

ADVANCED ATTACK

Demanding Play: You must have a well-balanced team, polished teamwork, fully developed individual skills, and a great deal of endurance to bring three hitters to the net.

The three-hitter offense is also described as the 6-0 system because, technically, everyone on the team is a hitter. Players move continuously from defensive to offensive positions. Although there are two designated setters in this system, there will be times during the rotation when setters must be hitters and times when a hitter must play the setter's role.

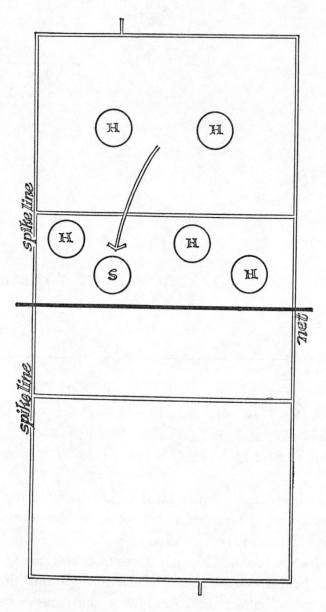

In the 6-0 attack, the setter runs from the back court to the net as soon as the serve is made. Three hitters at the net give the maximum offensive options.

It takes talented players who are willing to devote hours to practice.

Attack Force: Three hitters at the net gives a big advantage over the 4-2 system where you just have two. Blockers will be challenged time and again, and there will be many plays when they simply cannot meet the challenge.

Teams with a 6-0 attack position players in the line-up so that a setter is always in the back court no matter what stage the rotation.

Suppose at the start of the game the back-right player is a setter. The next player to the left will be a hitter, and the player at the back-left position will be one with all-around talent—a technique player. The player at front left will be the second setter. The player in the middle at the front will be the second hitter, and the player at front right will be the second technique player.

In this alignment, the front three players will be spikers. As the serve comes over the net, the back-court setter will run up from the right-back position in time to take the pass at the net and make the set to one of the three spikers. Then, if not needed to recover a blocked ball, the setter must leave the net quickly to help defend the back court.

As positions rotate clockwise, the first setter moves to middle court and plays the same system from there. As you can see, as rotation continues the front and back lines will always be made up of one setter, one technique player, and one hitter.

There will be plays when the back-court setter will be forced to receive serve. When this happens, the back-court technique player or sometimes the back-court hitter will run up to make the set. This switch occurs most often on serves that go to setters playing the back-left corner. It is difficult to run up from that position, reach the net and turn to face the on-hand hitter at the front left corner.

All these shifts require a system of team signals to avoid confusion. Even with signals, a team that has not scrimmaged together many times will still get crossed up.

Front Line: As the serve is made to your team, all three of the front-line players will be eligible hitters, one of them should be the first or second strongest hitter you have. Because many power hitters prefer the on-hand corner at the net, your hitters may shift positions as necessary after the serve. Crossing the width of the court, however, is not always possible, so the shift will often be on for some plays and off for others.

Blockers tend to lean toward the strong hitter's spot, and this can open up the court for the two other hitters. As the pass comes up from the back court to your setter, the hitters should move from the spiking line toward the net. Meanwhile, the setter, who has come up from the back court to the spot at net, must check the defensive alignment and decide on the attack.

If turned to the on-side area of the court, the setter will face the strong hitter at the corner and another hitter at the middle, either of whom will be ready for a forward set. The off-side hitter, behind the setter, will be ready for a back set.

The setter has further options in type of set—a standard set or a short one for a quick spike. In most cases, the middle hitter will have the best chance against blockers with a short set as a high set to the middle usually draws a three-blocker defense.

A short back set to the off-hand hitter will often catch the defense sleeping, particularly if the on-hand and middle hitters can fake to freeze the blockers. Making the short back set, however, is an extremely difficult play.

A short set that is two or three feet above the net— sometimes called a two set—will give the hitter the options of a hard or off-speed spike or a dink shot. Off-speed hits and dinks are usually not possible on the lower one sets that rise just a foot above the net.

After the hit, all other front-line players must be in position to back up the hitter and recover a blocked ball. This, technically, is part of team defense, but as already stated, offense and defense tend to flow together in volleyball. That's one of the things that makes the game so exciting.

Back Line: When the serve is made, all players on the court, with the exception of the designated setter who will be running to net position, must be prepared to receive and pass. Most serves, however, will be handled by one of the two players left in the back court.

These two players position themselves to cover the gaps between the three front-line hitters, forming a W pattern. This pattern is used by nearly all teams whether they are playing a 4-2 or a 6-o offense.

Servers will usually try to spot the ball deep to the sides or between the two back-line receivers. Receivers, obviously, must be alert and quick on their feet, and they must be ready to take over the setter's role if a fast serve to the setter forces him or her to make the pass.

Variation: Teams can make offensive adjustments to cover unbalanced distribution of talent and still put three hitters on the front line at least half the time. This variation is called the 5-1 attack. Very simply, it means that the team has just one designated setter instead of two.

When rotation puts this player in the back line, he or she will run up to position at the net and be able to dish the ball off to one of three hitters. When rotation puts the designated setter in the front line, however, your team will be limited to a two-hitter attack just as if you were playing a 4-2 system.

Even when you are playing a 6-o system, you may be forced to launch a two-hitter attack if the designated setter or an alternate setter is unable for some reason to reach the pass. This often happens when your team faces tough serves that lead to wild passing.

Tips

1. You must master all the individual skills and put in long hours of team practice to play an advanced offense.

2. Setters must use all the options to take full advantage of the 6-0 system. Repeated use of the same attack invites tight blocking.

3. Hitters must be ready at all times to fill in as setter if the designated setter should fail to get into position or be out of the play because of a bad pass.

4. While it is relatively easy for hitters who are facing the net to read defensive alignments, setters must use peripheral vision and sometimes rely on teammates' signals to put the ball in the best spot for a spike.

Defensive Strategy

7

BLOCKING

Front Line: Blocking is the front line of defense, and good blocking, like many other defensive plays in volleyball, can turn into an offensive play that will fatten your score.

Blocking requires both individual skill and teamwork. You must be extremely alert to reach the net at the right place at the right time, and you must know what part your teammates will take in the play. Even when you are blocking alone, you must try to force shots to the areas of your court that are covered by your teammates. This means that you must know where your teammates are, or at least where they are supposed to be.

59

Timing: Like spiking, timing is vital for good blocking. Unless you are very tall, you will have to make a short run into your jump, and you must go straight up to avoid hitting the net. Blockers can extend their hands over the net, but they must not touch it.

Jumping too soon or too late will take you out of the play completely. This is why some tall men who look impressive on the court sometimes can't block as well as shorter more agile players. If you can't time your jumps, you never will be an effective blocker even if you stand six, six in your stocking feet. It must be said, however, that height can be a terrific advantage when combined with good timing. A tall blocker with good jumping ability can go up for the ball with just one or perhaps no steps. This can be devastating against even the most powerful spikers.

How many steps you must take depends on your height and jumping ability. In any case, you will have to take fewer steps than the spiker in order to get up in time for the ball. You will not ordinarily go as high or hang in the air as long as the spiker because he or she has had a stronger run. This is why timing is so important. You must be there at the peak of your jump at the precise moment the spike is made.

Style: At the point of take-off, your knees should be bent and your cocked elbows should be at your sides so that both hands are up, even with your head. As you begin the jump, swing your elbows back, and then thrust your arms straight up as you flex your knees to make the lift.

Body positions for the block.

Your arms must go straight up, about fifteen inches apart to prevent shots through a gap over your head. Your hands should be extended, fingers and thumbs spread, but keep a slight bend in your fingers to prevent jamming from a hard-hit ball.

To improve the chance of taking the block off the heel of your hand, the best spot, cock your wrists back slightly so the heels point toward the ball. When you reach over the net, the heels of your hands will be fur-

61

Hand position for the block

ther exposed. When you start falling, bring your hands back quickly to avoid the net.

Blocking is too often neglected in practice. Do your workouts at the net so that you don't develop sloppy arm habits. Take off close enough to the center line to reach over the net without your hands or any other part of the body touching it.

Make sure you land with good balance, able to turn quickly to follow the play in your side of the court and be ready for your offensive role.

Teamwork: Three blockers on a spike make a very strong front line of defense, but mustering three players quickly enough at any spot other than the center of the net is almost impossible. This is one reason why most shots will be coming from the corners.

The end blocker sets the position for a two-blocker defense when the spike comes from the corner.

In team blocking the player first on the scene sets the position for the block. At the corners, for instance, the end blocker will decide the position, and it will be the middle blocker's responsibility to move sideways and join the block. For sets toward the middle, the middle blocker will anchor the position, and it will be up to one or both of the end players to position themselves in line.

The front-line players must do their best to put up a two-blocker defense. Four hands, properly spaced above the net will wall off a large portion of your court, and force the spiker to dink or try a tough angle shot.

The end blocker, whether working alone or with the middle blocker's help, must defend against the side-line shot by jumping from a spot close enough to the side line to cut the angle to the line. The end blocker, in other words, must position himself outside the hitter. If the hitter can gain the outside edge, he or she will have the choice of a side-line shot or a carom shot off the blocker's outside arm that will carry out of bounds.

In a three-blocker defense you must close the gap between the blockers that invites a shot into an unguarded area of your court. That gap will be open if the middle blocker has too slow a start for the ball and tries to jump too far from the end blocker.

The middle player must be able to move sideways rapidly, using either a crossover step or a series of quick side-steps. These moves have to be made while the blocker is giving all his attention to the opposing setter and hitters. If you as the middle blocker fail to close the gap, you will be out of the play, no use to your team.

You can often put up three blockers when sets go to the middle of the net.

Furthermore, your back-court players will mistakenly think there is more safe ground to leave unguarded than actually exists. Shout a warning if you can't close the gap.

Mistakes: Inexperienced blockers will often go up for shots that should be left for the back-court players. If the opposing setter has put up a poor pass, and you know that the player making the hit is not a good spiker, your team will be better off starting your offense with a back-court pass.

65

This is true of any weak shot. It is also true of most hard spikes hit far enough back from the net to give your back-court players time to position themselves for a good pass.

Another mistake beginning blockers often make is failing to jump close enough to the net. You want the ball to go back in your opponent's court. Block a few feet back from the net and the ball will fall into your court. Remember, a blocked ball in your court counts as the first of your team's hits. It will be tough for one of your teammates to dig the falling, blocked ball well enough to produce a good hit.

Good blockers concentrate on the opposing hitter as the play develops, not on the ball. The ball and the hitter will come together at the net, and by watching the hitter's approach you can get a good idea of his or her intentions.

Guidelines: As you gain experience, you will be able to learn the hitting traits of the opponents, be able to pick out the best and the weakest hitters on their team, and perhaps get clues from the hand and voice signals used during their offense.

If a hitter fails to jump high enough, you can usually expect an off-speed hit. Short sets on a quick attack almost always produce cross-court shots. An on-hand hitter will have a better chance for a line shot than an off-hand hitter. When a corner hitter fails to swing out of bounds on his or her approach, a line shot may be coming.

These are general rules, and clever hitters will cross you up by breaking them. Study individual traits constantly. Some hitters will not be good on short sets. Others favor just one or two angles while others seem able to spike in all directions. Share your observations with your teammates. It is vital that you work together.

Tips

1. Don't close your eyes or flinch away from a hit. Blocking is an aggressive play.

2. Let weak hits and spikes hit far from the net go to your back-court passers.

3. Watch the opposing hitter's approach. It gives you the best indication of hitting angle.

4. Try to play at least two blockers on every good spike.

5. Study the traits of the opposing hitters and setters. Do your best, as the game progresses, to learn what their hand and voice signals mean.

6. End blockers are responsible for positioning the team block at the corners. The middle blocker sets the mid-net block.

7. Jump close enough to the net to block the ball into your opponent's court. It takes practice to do this without touching the net.

8. Blocking is the first line of defense.

8

DIGGING

The Big Edge: Games in top-level volleyball are won on defense. Your offensive play will not mean much if your defense is out-matched by the opposition. When the opposition dives and rolls to dig your hardest spikes or stuffs them back in your court with expert blocking, there will be no way you can pull off a victory without putting up an equally strong defense of your own.

Of course, it's fun to spike the ball, but don't let fun interfere with a balanced development of skill. A little playing experience will show you that there is just as much fun and satisfaction in saving a point as there is in making one, and when back-court players can dig the ball time and time again, your team will have a second line of defense that will cool off the hottest spikers in a hurry.

Rolling: To fall to the floor safely and reach the ball either with a dive or a roll, you must master the art of

The roll

the tumbler. Many coaches and physical education experts discourage such plays for youngsters. Some say that the risk of injury is too great for players under fifteen years of age.

This limit is rather arbitrary. There are too many exceptional young players, particularly among the girls, who are agile and adept enough to learn the tumbling skills much earlier. Follow this rule. If you are fifteen or somewhat younger, begin working on these skills under the close supervision of a qualified coach. Even if you are older but have some tendency toward awkwardness or simply lack confidence, good coaching will give you a safe start.

Playing lawn or beach volleyball is also a good way to initiate yourself to the dive and rolling digs without high risk of injury.

There are basically two rolls, the side or shoulder roll and the back roll. The back roll is used when you must run backward and then crouch low to get under the ball, either with a pass off your spread fingers or a bump off your forearms. The momentum of your run will carry your body backward off balance. If you are in a good low squat to begin with, there will be little impact when your buttocks hit the floor, but you must not sit back squarely with a stiff back as if you were dropping into a chair.

Instead, cushion the impact on one buttock and let the backward momentum carry you into a roll. Sometimes you will go all the way over on your shoulders into a backward somersault and be able to hop up from your hands and knees. Other times, when momentum hasn't been as great, you will rock back from your shoulders and either come straight up with your feet under you or roll sideways, using your hands to push yourself onto your feet.

Recovery must be quick to bring you back in the game, but you must always roll enough to absorb momentum. Most injuries occur when the player does not go into the roll with a deep enough knee squat. You should be practically sitting on your heels when you begin your fall. You must also avoid the temptation to reach back, trying to stop the roll with your hands or elbows. That can cause painful bruises. So too can a hard sit-down squarely on the tail bone.

In practicing all falling plays, it is important to work without a ball until the tumbling moves become almost instinctive to you. Most of your conscious effort must be focused on the ball and on getting it up for a teammate. This is not easy. Whether you make a bump pass or an overhand pass, nearly all the power must come from your arms. You are not likely to get much distance on the ball, but in a desperation play, your main concern is to put the ball up so that a teammate can come in and pass it to one of your hitters.

The Side Roll: This follows a one- or two-arm bump pass made on the run far to one side. Because you had to run or at least lunge to reach the ball, your momen-

The side roll

tum will take you into a fall. In many plays you may be off balance and going down when you make your pass. Try to keep your balance as long as possible by maintaining a low center of gravity. This is best done by dropping to the knee on your hitting side just as you make your hit.

The knee will provide a platform long enough for you to maintain balance and aim your hit. Usually, a player can get more distance and control with a hit off a side roll than a back roll. However, the same rule applies for both plays. Your first concern is to get the ball up.

After hitting the ball, your momentum will carry you into the roll. Bend your knees fully as you go down and let the thigh of the leg on the hitting side cushion your impact. Tuck both elbows into your chest so that no parts of your hands or arms slap the floor.

As the roll continues, the area of floor contact should move smoothly from thigh to buttock to back and shoulders. At the same time, lift your legs, well bent at the hips. Let your feet arc over you, as you rock to your shoulders.

At this point, when most of your weight will be riding on your shoulders, your head will probably be toward the net, with you looking at the ceiling. Let the roll continue.

As your legs come over you, tuck your knees so that your opposite thigh cushions you and lets you come up, with an arm assist if necessary onto your knees. From that position, you are ready to hop up and get back into action.

Done properly, the side roll is one of the prettiest moves in the game. Your teammates and your fans will cheer your effort. Your opponents across the net, however, may not be so enthusiastic, particularly if you consistently save points for your team.

The Dive: Another spectacular play, the dive, is used to reach balls ahead of you, either directly ahead or slightly to one side. These are balls you cannot reach without making a strong run and a leap into the air. Your hit can be made with one or both arms. If you can use both arms, they should be in the bump-pass position, hands cupped together.

The dive

While you may get a safe hit off your hands, try to take the ball just above your wrists. When you make your hit, you may be completely off the floor, sailing for-

74

ward. So immediately after putting the ball up, bring your arms down to take the first impact of your fall on your hands. Cushion the fall by bending the elbows and arching your back. You will be in a push-up position, sliding forward on your stomach and thighs. The slide will bring your shoulders forward between your hands. As your slide comes to a stop you can straighten your elbows and bring your feet under you to stand up.

The dive may be the most difficult play for you to master. Begin practicing with moderate jumps so you can learn the landing technique. Once you can make smooth landings you can start making big leaps with confidence and begin practicing with a ball.

Tips

1. Practice individual defensive skills without the ball until you can tumble with confidence and without a lot of conscious effort. When you begin working with the ball, you can give full attention to your hit.

2. Back rolls and side rolls are just that, rolls that absorb body momentum. Arms and hands should not be used to block the roll until momentum is all but spent.

3. The primary concern in these defensive plays is saving the ball, getting it up so a teammate can handle it. Don't spoil the play by trying to make an impossible pass.

4. If you are young, still growing, and going through some of the awkwardness of rapid growth, let an expert decide when you are ready to start these tumbling plays.

5. Lawn or beach volleyball may provide the best introduction to a tumbling defense.

9

RECEIVING SERVE

Whose Ball?: The player who receives serve must think about offense and defense at the same time. A mistake can lead to a direct loss of a point or else handicap your offense so badly that it leads to an indirect loss of point.

Referees tend to watch serve receivers closely for held balls. This is why the bump pass has replaced the overhead pass almost entirely on this play. If the receiver commits a held ball or a double hit, the other team wins an easy point.

You must play the ball cleanly, and you must get your pass up where your setter can handle it accurately.

Positions: The majority of serves come to the middle third of the court, the area ten feet back from the net and ten feet up from the end line. Good servers, however, can place the ball deeper. Thus, you must have at least one player well back near the end line to handle the deep balls. Most teams function best, however, with two players deep.

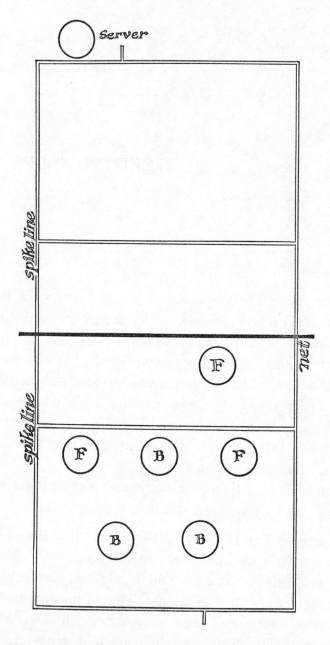

The W-serve-receiving pattern works for either the 4-2 or 6-0 offense. In the 4-2 offense, the setter will already be at the net when the serve is made. In the 6-0 offense, the setter will run up from the back court.

The W pattern has already been described. Here the designated setter is either moving toward the net or already stationed there. Three of the other five players should be stationed across mid-court with the two remaining players back, filling the gaps between the three in front to form the W.

In the 4-2 offense, with one of the front players at the net as setter, the other two front players—your two hitters—will be on the side lines at the wings of the W. They move up when the set is made. The mid-back-court player will come forward to the peak of the W. In the 6-0 offense, the designated setter will be moving up from the back line, and your three hitters will be at the top points of the W.

Another receiving pattern that can be used in the 4-2 offense calls for an arching deployment of the five back players with the three back-court players guarding the back third of the court and the hitters at each end guarding the middle side lines. It is like the W pattern except the peak player in the W has moved back to form a cuplike receiving line.

This defense seems to work best for players who have had limited team workouts and are not sure of the assignments or the abilities of their teammates.

No matter what pattern you use, never take up positions that screen a receiver. All players must have a clear view of the server and the ball. Another important point is the signal. When the ball comes to you, call for it. Shout, "I've got it!" or "Mine!"—anything to keep an eager teammate from interfering with your play.

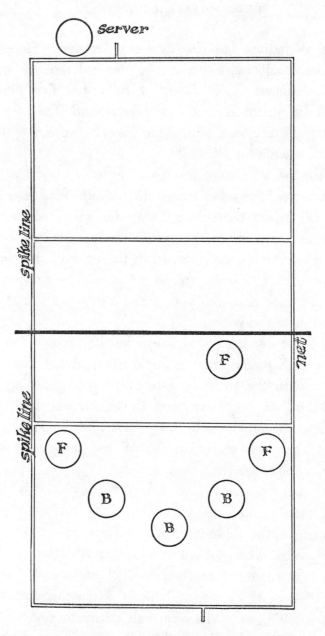

The cup defense against the serve works well for teams without much experience. No matter what pattern you use, make sure all players can see the server and the ball.

Staying Loose: You will often see games in which a trailing team makes a remarkable comeback on serve. Many times this can be traced to a build up of tension among the receivers. They start worrying about the score, begin moving stiffly, and passing poorly.

You must stay loose. Stand on the balls of your feet, weight well forward, and arms in front of you. Be ready to move in any direction. If you are not the receiver, you must move to your offensive position. Back players, in fact, should already be thinking of their defensive assignments.

The team must flow with the ball. Confusion about where you should be, what you should do will not only make you ineffective but will also interfere with and confuse your teammates.

The Hot Server: Maybe you and your teammates don't tense up, but the opposing server simply gets a streak going. With each point, the server's confidence will mount, and the serves seem to grow sharper and harder for you to handle. Check your positions.

Remember, a good server will try to make you back up to pass the ball. He or she will also try to shave the side lines or drop the ball close to the end line, hoping that you will hesitate in deciding whether or not to play the ball.

Look at your position in relation to the lines before play begins and decide what path an out ball will take in relation to your body. Anything inside or lower than that path will be a ball that must be played. On close balls, it is generally better to play safe. When an untouched serve nicks the line, the opponents win a point.

Tips

1. Receiving serve is the defensive play that starts your offense.

2. Avoid fouls that will cost a point. Pass the ball cleanly.

3. No matter what receiving pattern your team uses, always make sure that all players have a clear view of the server and the ball.

4. If you are taking serve, call for it so that your teammates can move to their offensive positions.

5. Don't tense up. Stay loose, on the balls of your feet, ready to move.

6. An accurate server will aim for the corners and try to shave the lines. Be aware of your position in relation to the lines before each serve.

7. It is always better to take the close ball rather than hesitate or guess wrong on a liner.

10
DEFENSIVE PATTERNS

Working System: Your team can experiment with defense. Certainly, you should be prepared to make adjustments to handle special situations, but at the start of play and throughout most games, you will be on safe and solid ground with a 2-4 system of defense.

It calls for two blockers on the front line and four players back to dig the ball. Even with two blockers doing their job well, there will be a big expanse of court for the four diggers to cover. They must position themselves so responsibility for coverage is evenly distributed. Let's examine these positions and their responsibilities during the most common attack in the game, a ball set to the on-hand hitter (a right-hander) at the right side of your net.

Back Right: The player at this position will have two primary concerns, a dink shot over the blockers or a shot down the line. If your end blocker does not stay outside the hitter, the spike down the line will be open. To see how well your blocker is guarding the line, you must stand practically on it. You should be up about eight feet from the end line, far enough forward to get up for the dink, yet deep enough to handle a hard line spike. If from your side-line position you have a clear view of the hitter, you will know that your end blocker has left the lane open for a line shot. In this case, you will be frozen in position, unable to move until the hit is made.

On the other hand, if the end blocker does the job properly and closes the lane, you can move forward a few steps to be in better position for the dink before any hit is made.

Back Middle: Most coaches will tell you that this is the toughest defensive position to learn. You must play deep, at the end line or a step behind it. You can run up to retrieve deep dinks from there, and you can also dig hard middle spikes, but your toughest job will be playing balls that come back to you off your own blockers.

You cannot let these balls go out of bounds because your team had the last touch. Also, since the hit off the blocker counted as your team's first hit, you must try to set the ball from your deep position.

Middle players, worried about the big expanse of court in front of them, tend to come forward too far. This forces them to run back to save those blocked balls. Though you might get the ball in the air, it is almost impossible for anyone to set the ball accurately while moving backward. Stay back so you can move up on the ball.

Back Left: Since spikers get their greatest power by hitting angle shots down and away from the on-hand side, the back defender on the left side of the court must be prepared to dig.

The hard, cross-court spike, actually, will not be too difficult for a defender with average ability provided he or she holds good position and is able to move quickly to the ball. Usually, the biggest problem for newcomers in this position comes with the softer, mid-court spikes. In most cases, these should be left for the middle defender.

Some coaches recommend that the back-left player stand about ten feet from the back line and five feet from the side line with the understanding that the player will take no balls hit to his or her right side. The middle defender will be responsible for those hits. This avoids collisions or a ball that slams untouched to the floor between two confused defenders.

In any case, defenders must agree before play begins just who will take responsibility for hits to the back-left-player's right side.

Left Front: As one of the three front-line blockers, the player in this position becomes the end blocker when the set is made to the off-hand hitter. With a set to the on-hand hitter, however, the player must fill a crucial role in the four-digger defense.

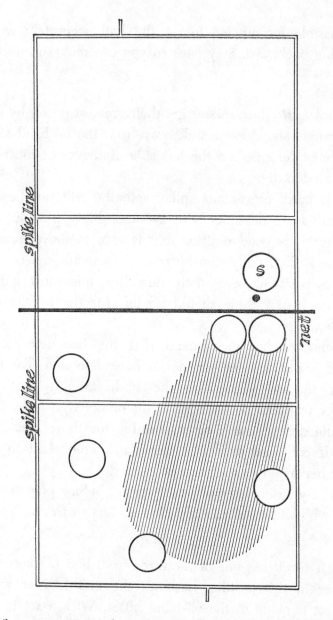

When a set goes to the on-hand hitter on the right side of the opposite court, you should defend against the hard spike with this pattern. The shaded area shows the "safe" area of your court that you can expect behind a good, two-blocker defense.

When your team has good blocking, the on-hand hitter's only shot may be one that takes a sharp, cross-court angle close to the net. The left-front player must stand about six feet back from the net and two feet from the side line and be prepared to dig any low spike. Hits that come to this player above the hips, however, will be out of bounds. Let these go, and your team will win a point or a side out.

A smart hitter will try to keep you off balance by mixing cross-court dinks in with the barrage of hard spikes. Again, you and your blockers must agree beforehand which dinks are your responsibility. The middle blocker usually will take dinks to your right while the back-court players will take dinks over the blockers' heads.

Of course, when the set is made close to the middle of the net, all front-line players should try to put up a three-blocker line. Back-court players will have less court to cover behind three blockers, but they must be prepared for hits off the blockers. The most common pattern calls for the middle player to move up to take dink shots hit over the blockers' heads and for the side players to come in about fifteen feet from the end line, ready to run up for angled shots or dinks or move back for deep spikes toward the corners.

No Blockers: When the other team makes a poor set deep in the court, your team's defense must become offense oriented to take advantage of the volley or deep spike that is almost sure to come into your court.

Usually, a back-court player will call a signal to cancel the block. When this happens, the front-line players must take a few steps back from the net, and back-court players, with the exception of the one playing the left-back position, must take a few steps forward.

When your designated setter runs up before the other team makes its hit, vacating a back-court position, your team must make a shift to cover the gap. The back-middle player, for instance, may have to move to the right while the front players come back to form the W-pattern defense.

All this should happen on the setter's signal, usually "Coming in," or simply, "In." Mix-ups on the shift can destroy your offensive advantage.

Other Patterns: Your team should be prepared to alter its defense for special situations. For instance, if your opponents have poor spikers or are simply winning points with clever off-speed hits and dinks, you might move one of the back players up about ten feet behind the blockers, to their left for on-hand hitters and to their right for off-hand hitters.

This leaves the two remaining back-court players responsible for deep spikes to the corners and angle shots toward the side lines. You can establish the same pattern by moving the off-blocker in to back up the blockers and bringing a back-court player up to cover the off-blocker's side of the court.

You must also be prepared for blocking break-downs. Suppose a short set goes to the middle and your middle blocker is the only one able to jump in time. This leaves your two end blockers out of action for the moment. Your back-court players at the sides must come up to cover the angled spike while the middle player must stay back for a deep spike. In addition, all back-court players must be on the lookout for off-speed hits or dinks.

Tips

1. The position of the set and the effectiveness of your blockers determine your defensive positioning.

2. Co-ordination is vital. Use voice signals, and make pregame plans of coverage to avoid mistakes.

3. The first sign of a poorly prepared team will show on defense. It takes hours of team practice to put up an effective defense.

4. Be prepared to alter your defense for special situations.

5. Alertness is vital. You must know where your opponents are, where the ball is going, and what areas of the court you and your teammates will cover.

6. A no-blocker defense should put your team into an immediate offensive pattern. One player should be responsible for calling the blockers "down."

Physical and Mental Preparation

11
LEVELS OF PLAY

Recreation Play: Volleyball does not have to be a pressure game. That's one of the best things about it. It can provide exercise and stimulation for workers during a luncheon break. It can give schoolyard fun either during recess or after classes. It can be pursued more as a social experience than a sport.

The number of players on a side may vary greatly. Although twelve to a side may qualify as jungle ball, it is still fun. Inexperience will not limit the fun greatly. If a player can hit an underhand serve and handle basic passing responsibilities, he or she can have fun with everyone else in an informal game.

93

Volleyball used to be the one sport where players called their own fouls. This is no longer the case in serious competition, but the tradition certainly should continue in informal games.

Okay, suppose you have worked hard to develop your skills and you want to test those skills in serious competition. That's great, but don't turn your back on the fun of informal games.

Get out and play. You will work on your individual skills and keep yourself fit. You will enjoy the social aspects of volleyball. You will relax and have fun. And chances are that, like many experienced players, you will find great satisfaction in introducing the game to others. It is a real kick to see a newcomer's interest and enthusiasm grow. One day you may introduce the game to someone who turns into a star player. You will indeed take pride in that.

Cautions: There are a few necessary words of warning about the informal game. You must recognize the level of play, and be aware of the skills of the other players. Obviously, you should not drive hard spikes at some inept player who is trying to discover the fun of the game. If you must spike, pick out an opponent who has the skill and experience to dig the ball. Don't run others on your side off the ball. If the court is not too crowded with players, play your position and encourage your teammates to do likewise.

Although the game may be informal, don't let it lead you into bad habits. Individual skills can be polished in any kind of game as long as you have a regulation ball and a tight net.

Competitive Play: Standard, six-on-a-side games are not the only serious games in volleyball. Two-on-a-side beach volleyball is very serious business on the beaches of Southern California where tournaments are held nearly every weekend and where play-off games draw two to three thousand spectators.

There is also tournament play for coed volleyball which is enjoying a big surge in popularity. Coed volleyball, obviously, provides good social experience when played informally, and when played seriously, it becomes an excellent spectator sport as the professional leagues have discovered. The pro teams are now composed of four men and two women.

No matter what kind of game you play, if competition is serious, you must do your very best. You owe that to yourself, your teammates and your coach.

Winning Attitude: Let's face it, competition is the only way to measure individual and team skills. And if you want to win, you must be able to take pressure and you must be willing to work very hard.

Some people simply do not have the personality for competition. They may enjoy participation, but the emphasis on winning will never suit their characters. There is certainly nothing wrong with this. But it is a sad situation when such people are forced into competition by parental or peer pressure. The game that was once fun becomes an ordeal to them. They develop a negative attitude which can be damaging both to themselves and their teammates.

Don't let this happen to you. Before you become involved in competitive play, ask yourself if it is really what you want. Actually, most of us love to compete. In fact, Americans have been accused of taking their games too seriously. Perhaps this is true, but the volleyball court is not the place to debate the matter, not if you and your teammates are playing to win.

Just make sure when you go out for the team that you are not making the effort to satisfy or please someone else, that it is your idea and your idea alone.

Dedication: For the competitive level of play, you must attain and maintain peak fitness. This calls for a routine of daily exercise that must include plenty of running or other vigorous activity that builds heart and lung stamina.

The pace of volleyball is demanding. If you begin to tire during those closing minutes of a game, you will be letting your teammates down just when they need you most. To stay in condition for volleyball you should run or jog at least two miles a day for at least three days a week. Most players follow a more intense routine.

You must do other exercises both to stretch and strengthen muscles. Some exercises will strengthen your jumping and hitting ability. Others can improve your balance and reflexes. Specific exercises will be discussed in the next chapter.

In addition to work on your own fitness program, you must practice with your team, polishing your individual skills and learning the fine art of team play. This usually means two to three hours every day during the weeks of the volleyball season.

Do you have the dedication let alone the time for this kind of schedule?

Fun at the Top: Like any other activity in life, the more you put into a sport, the more you will get out of it. Don't get the idea that your hard work and dedication will spoil the fun of competitive volleyball. Instead, it will increase your enjoyment a hundred fold.

There is great satisfaction in knowing that you played your very best, that you and your teammates took advantage of every opportunity, and that you made your own opportunities with well-planned tactics.

And there is really no end to this. The more you play, the better you will become. So make no mistake, serious competition, if you are suited for it, is the best level of play there is.

Tips

1. Skillful, experienced players should not overpower an informal game. Adjust to the level of play, concentrate on individual skills, and have fun.

2. Don't let your friends or your family pressure you into competition. Make sure it is what you want before you take it up.

97

3. Serious volleyball calls for hard work and dedication. Make sure you are willing to give 100 per cent.

4. The more skillful you become as an individual and as a team, the more pleasure and satisfaction you can expect from the game.

12

CONDITIONING

Special Needs: An exercise program that keeps you fit is a must for any sport. Strong and pliant muscles, good balance, quick reflexes, and stamina are beneficial for everyone, but a volleyball player must also have exceptional jumping ability and exceptional endurance.

The conditioning requirements are similar to those for basketball. Basketball players run a great deal. So, too, do volleyball players. Running or some other activity that maintains a high pulse and high breathing rate over a period of several minutes must be part of your training. Cycling at a good speed, skipping rope, jogging or jogging in place, distance swimming, and brisk walking all help improve the efficiency of the heart and lungs.

These activities also strengthen leg muscles, but volleyball players must do some special exercises to build muscles that give legs that explosive jumping power.

Heart and Lungs: Working muscles burn fuel and produce waste, and the fuel cannot be turned into energy without oxygen. Reduce the supply of fuel and oxygen or let waste accumulate, and the muscles will simply stop working, perhaps even knot up in painful cramps.

The lungs take in oxygen and eliminate waste in the form of carbon dioxide, while the circulatory system, with the heart as the pump, distributes the oxygen along with the fuel processed by the digestive system to all tissues of the body. Obviously, all the organs involved including the arteries and veins of the circulatory system must have top capacity and be in top condition to meet the demands of an active game like volleyball. Top capacity and condition can be attained only through vigorous use of the organs involved.

Surprisingly, few team sports exercise the organs sufficiently to do the job because action is rarely sustained long enough to build the capacity of the heart and lungs.

Lack of capacity and condition shows quickly in volleyball, particularly during tournament play when teams compete on a best-of-three or best-of-five schedule. When a team that looked sharp in its first game falls apart in the crucial closing games, you can be pretty sure that the players neglected their roadwork.

Whether you run, cycle, or swim, make sure that the workout involves sustained exertion, and that you follow a regular schedule. Perhaps three heavy workouts a week will suit your needs, or maybe shorter, daily workouts will fit better into your routine. Whatever program you adopt, stick to it even in the off season. You might be able to strengthen arm or leg muscles in a preseason crash program, but heart and lung conditioning cannot be done quickly.

In fact, if you are out of shape or just starting a training program, you must begin gradually, jogging or running just a few minutes a day, and building your workouts slowly as your capacity and conditioning improve.

Jumping: Deep knee bends always prompt controversy among physical fitness instructors. Certainly, if you have a knee injury or defect, you should avoid the exercise, and if you are still growing you should do deep bends only after your coach or trainer has given approval.

Although the exercise can aggravate an injury or point up a defect, deep knee bends should be included in the healthy player's training program. Many volleyball players do knee bends with weights, but don't start this unless you have your full physical growth with well-muscled legs.

The deep bending and flexing of the knees is required for jumping at the net, particularly for blocking when you must get up with little or no approach. You must also bend knees to get down for digging and passing. If you are developed enough to use weights—a coach can help you decide—remember that it is the number of repetitions of the exercise not the amount of weight that is important.

While knee bends will strengthen muscles, actual jumping will give them explosive power. Face a wall and do stationary jumps from a deep squat, bringing both arms up to touch the wall as high as you can, just as if you were putting up a block. The wall will make you perform vertical jumps cleanly without a touch, and by marking your maximum height on the wall with a piece of chalk, you can measure your weekly progress.

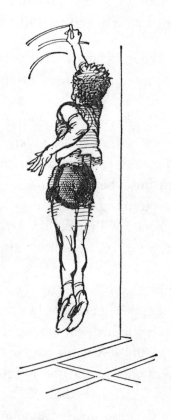

Practicing the jump

Sprinting, jumping in track and field sports, and basketball will help build explosive leg power. Many basketball players take up volleyball as a retirement or post-season activity. Wilt Chamberlain says it is now his favorite sport.

Other Exercises: Standard strengthening and limbering exercises such as push-ups, sit-ups, chinning, bends, twists, groin stretches, and many of the stretching exercises of yoga can be worked into your conditioning program to fit your personal needs. You must have strong arms and shoulders and a strong abdomen to make those hard spikes, and you must be limber for all the action of volleyball.

No matter what your daily routine, be sure you do loosening up exercises before every game and practice session. This will not only improve your reaction time, but it will also help prevent muscle pulls. Stretch your legs with bends and knee pulls and a good groin stretching exercise. The hurdler's stretch, done in a sitting position with one leg forward and the other bent back while you alternately touch the toe of the extended foot will stretch the groin and prevent a painful injury during game action. You can also stand with feet apart and alternately bend one leg deeply and then the other, forcing a good stretch along the inside of the extended leg.

Reflex and Balance: Tumbling has already been cited as good preparation for the diving and rolling moves of volleyball. The sport also helps develop reflexes and balance.

A workout on a speed punching bag will improve hand-eye reflexes and timing. Simple balancing exercises, such as knee bends with a book on your head, standing toe lifts with your eyes closed, and one-leg ballet stands will also help you develop balance and body control.

When you begin training for the game under the guidance of a good coach, you will undoubtedly do several exercises at the start of each practice session. When these duplicate things you have been doing at home, you can adjust your home workouts accordingly. Just make sure you know your individual needs. If your arms lack striking power, for instance, retain push-ups or pull-ups in your daily, home routine.

Tips

1. Top efficiency of the heart and the lungs is the key to physical stamina. Include running, jogging, distance swimming, or some other sustained activity in your regular workouts.

2. Begin running or jogging gradually. It takes time to build stamina.

3. Knee bends and jumping exercises will increase your jumping height, but you must work on form as well so that you will jump cleanly without touching the net.

4. Other exercises that strengthen and loosen muscles can be included in your workouts according to individual need.

5. Muscle-loosening and -stretching exercises should also be part of prepractice and pregame workouts.

6. Like muscle strength, reflex and balance can be improved through exercise. Tumbling provides good training for volleyball.

7. If you have special problems, ask a coach to help you plan your fitness program. If you are still growing, don't start training with weights without a coach's supervision.

13

TEAM DRILLS

Organized Fun: Practice sessions should be fun, but if they are to do any good at all, they must be organized. When you work out without the supervision of a coach, someone on your team, either the captain or an experienced player, should plan the practice sessions.

One or two unplanned practices should be enough to drive this point home. Without organization there is no benefit, and unless you thrive on chaos, there will be no fun.

Even with a coach, practice will give little benefit when there is no planning. In fact, many players judge coaches by their practice sessions. A good coach will know what must be emphasized, which players need encouragement, which need extra work on certain skills, and how time should be divided between work on individual skills, team drills, and scrimmaging. Let's look at some typical drills.

Pair Jumping: With the squad in two lines on either side of the net, the first players in each line should jump to touch hands over the net. After the first jump, each moves sideways two steps and jumps again while the next players come up to jump. At the end of the net, the players form another line, ready to jump and move in the other direction.

This drill is excellent for timing and explosive leg power. It also gives your coach a chance to check your jumping form.

Pass-set: Four players station themselves at four corners of their court. Since the ball never passes over the net, another group of four can be doing this drill simultaneously on the other side of the net. One of the back players sets the ball up to the on-hand spiker who jumps to set the ball to the off-hand spiker. He or she then sets the ball back to the on-hand corner, and the player there passes the ball to a back-court player, who starts the rotation again by setting to the off-hand spiker.

This is an excellent ball-handling drill, and it gives back-court players practice in making forward sets to the hitters, something that is often done during a game when the ball is dug defensively in the back court.

108

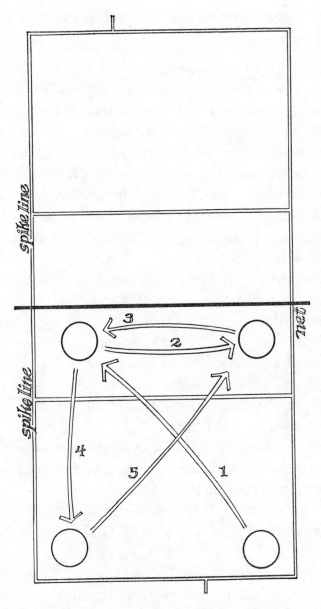

The pass-set drill

Players should rotate so that everyone practices at least once at each position.

Spiking: There are several ways to practice spiking. You can involve the entire team by lining up two groups of hitters in each court with a setter stationed at the net on each side. A hitter takes his or her turn by passing the ball to the setter and then running up to make a hit off the setter's ball. The hitter then runs around to the other court to shag balls and wait for another turn. Hitters trade off with setters to give everyone a chance, and after working on on-hand hits, the lines should move over for off-hand hits.

Another drill for spikers can be run as a team contest. A passer feeds the ball to a setter, who puts it up for the spiker. After the hit, another ball is put up immediately, and the spiker hits again, trying to continue the sequence of hits for as long as possible without a miss or a slowdown. When the spiker fails to make a good hit, another player becomes the hitter. Twenty or more consecutive spikes is a good score.

This drill takes lots of time if everyone on the team is to have a chance, and you also need several balls and ball shaggers to keep up the fast pace.

Still another spiking drill can be run with two players, a spiker, and a digger. The idea is to keep the ball in motion for as long as possible, much like a game of pepper in baseball. The spiker hits to the digger who must put the ball up for another hit. This gives the digger good practice with the bump pass. Roles should

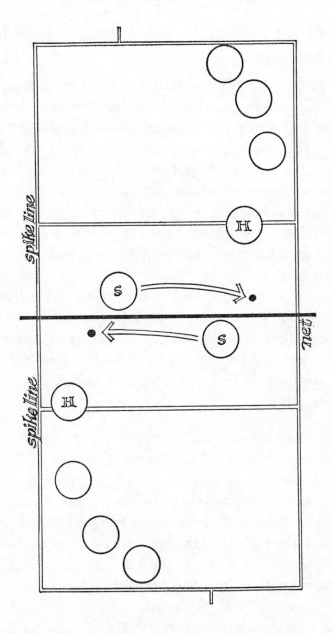

The line-up for the spiking drill with players at the ends of the lines helping to shag balls.

be changed from time to time to balance the workout for both players.

Setting Drill: Though the setter can benefit from the first two spiking drills described above, the players must practice making sets to all areas of the net, trying to imitate game conditions as much as possible. If your team uses a 6-0 offense, the setter must practice coming up from the back court to make the set.

Some coaches drill setters by lining up hitters along both side lines so that the set can be either forward or back, with the coach often calling the shot while the pass is in the air.

Passing overhand against a wall is a good individual workout for setters. You need a precise touch to make the ball bounce back the right distance and height for you to get under it for another pass. See how long you can keep the ball in action with clean against-the-wall passes.

Blocking: Players should form two lines, one in each court, with the head of the line at the middle of the net. Two hitters are positioned on chairs at opposite corners of the net. At a double signal such as, "Set—Block!" the lead player in each line moves over quickly and jumps to block the ball. After the block, the players run around to the back of the line in the other court, and help to shag balls until their turns come again.

This drill should be varied with double blocking, using two lines in each court so that one player is stationed at the corner and the other starts from the middle. The coach or other teammates must watch this drill closely to make sure that the players jump together and space their hands properly for an effective block.

When blockers start to tire, they can take a turn hitting on the chair.

Serving: Don't neglect the serve. Here's a drill that will provide practice in both making and receiving serve. Use a full team on the receivers' side. Have the server practice a full variety of serves to several different locations while the receiving team passes, sets, and spikes the ball back.

You will need three or four ball shaggers on the server's side to keep the drill moving briskly. This drill is better than individual serving practice in which one player ties up the entire court and gives the ball retriever little benefit.

Other Drills: There are, of course, many more drills. Some are simply variations on the basic ones described here. Others are special drills dreamed up by individual coaches to cure a special problem. Generally, a practice session should be built on a variety of drills, and new drills should be introduced frequently to build interest.

Some coaches, however, will use a single drill to drive home a lesson in tactics or overcome a team weakness. Focus on a weakness with a long, hard drill may come after a loss or string of losses suffered by your team. No matter what methods your coach uses, make the team drills count. The benefit you receive depends entirely on the effort you put into the drill.

Scrimmaging: The same can be said of the scrimmage. You should play just as hard in a scrimmage as you do in an actual game, but in most cases your coach should be prepared to stop the action for constructive criticism whenever mistakes are made. Some coaches let the game finish before holding a rap session, but beginning players particularly seem to learn faster when their errors draw an immediate whistle. And there will be great satisfaction when your team can finally play well enough to keep the whistle silent through a full game.

Tips

1. Practice drills should simulate game action as much as possible, and positions should rotate so that all players receive equal benefit.

2. Emphasis should be decided by your coach or an experienced player who is aware of weaknesses and knows best how to correct them.

3. A well-run drill is both hard work and good fun. Be a willing worker, and you and your teammates are almost sure to have fun.

4. Don't neglect serving drills. You cannot develop a variety of serves without experimentation and practice.

14

GAME PLAN

Team Line-up: Because you cannot alter your line-up during a game except through substitution, you must make sure that you will have at least one of your top hitters in the front line no matter what the stage of your rotation. The designated setters must also be properly spaced, and you should consider your defensive line-up as well.

If possible try to arrange your line-up so that your best blockers will go against the opposing team's best hitters, and your best passers will be in the back court against the opponent's best servers. This requires advanced knowledge of the opposing team.

Scouting: Game plans for almost all serious competition are now founded on thorough scouting reports. While it's true that you can and should watch other teams in action whenever you can during day-long tournament play, you will need sufficient knowledge far enough in advance so that you can go to the tournament with a definite plan for each team you meet.

There are many things to consider. For instance, if the opponents are known for their fine blocking, you must consider short sets or dink shots as part of your offensive strategy.

Should your blockers try to force shots down the line by cutting off the angle shots? It might be good strategy if opposing hitters have lots of power but little accuracy.

Where should the serve go? Aim for the weak passers whenever they have back-court positions.

Are there other weaknesses on the opposing team? If so, how can your team take advantage of those weaknesses?

Because scouting is so important in competitive volleyball, a scout will list every play on charts that rate passing, setting, spiking, blocking, and digging of each player. The reports also tell location of serve, the number of out serves, direction of spikes, the number of out spikes, blocking tactics—including areas covered by the block—and the number and type of fouls committed by each player.

Details can win points. For example, a blocker known to touch the net occasionally may give up points on fouls if your team is able to spike at this blocker repeatedly.

Coaches or their assistants usually do the scouting, but you should make up scouting reports on your own whenever the opportunity arises. The mental exercise will make you a more observant, more intelligent player.

Court Choice: When your team wins the coin toss before the start of a game or tournament, your captain must decide if you will get choice of court or choice of serve. Although it is important to open a game with the serve and the chance to score first, the choice of court can sometimes be more important, particularly if the game is being played outside where wind and sun can be problems.

Even indoors, windows can cause glare or uneven court lighting, and sometimes low beams, particularly near the net, can get in the way of a pass and cause you a side out or loss of point.

If conditions are equal on both sides of the net, however, you should always take the opportunity to serve first. This is particularly important in tournament play when decisions are based on an odd number of games, either best out of three or best out of five. Winning the toss means that your team will start serving in the first and the last game.

Time Out: You are allowed two, 30-second time outs per game. Each time out called in excess of two will cost a point. Any player or the coach can call the time out, but most teams have a rule that only the coach or team captain makes the call.

Best reason for calling time is to break an opposing server's scoring string. Points in volleyball tend to come in strings, so a time out can be effective in cooling off a hot offense. A coach can also use the time out to give instructions on strategy. In the heat of a game, what you hear in thirty seconds may make a bigger impression on you than anything you have heard from your coach repeatedly through hours of practice. A good coach knows this and turns time outs into instructive sessions for the players.

Substitutions: It takes bench strength to use substitutions as a strategic weapon. If a tired player must come out for a weak substitute, the advantage goes to the other team.

A good coach rarely waits until any of his players are exhausted before making substitutions. The coach knows each player's capabilities well, and if someone is not performing up to his or her capabilities, a substitution is in order.

Even the best players have bad days. A setter's timing might be off. Your ace server may have lost the fine touch. A blocker's reflexes may go lax. The coach must be able to spot the trouble and make the right changes early before the opponents have run up an insurmountable lead.

Substitutes should always warm up before going into a game, and they should know how to report to the scorer's table and get onto the court as soon as the ball is dead to avoid a time-out charge.

Signals: There should not be a great deal of chatter during the action, but you will need a set of prearranged signals to function as a team. Obviously, when you take a serve it is a good idea to call for it even if there is not another teammate nearby. Always make the call if there is a possibility of a collision.

If your pass for the setter is not on target, call out the error at once, saying either "Right," "Left," or "Back," as the case may be. This will give the setter and the hitters warning, and if some other player must make the set, he or she can start moving for the ball at once.

Setters often use number signals or some other code to tell where the ball is going, but these have to be fully disguised and changed frequently to keep opponents in the dark.

Back-court defenders usually have the best position for judging the need for a block, but just one player should be responsible for calling the blockers off. Otherwise, you may have conflicting calls when the opponents make a mediocre set, and your blockers will become hopelessly confused.

Tips

1. Scouting is necessary in preparing any workable game plan. You cannot even set your line-up to best advantage if you don't know who the strong spikers are on the other team.

2. Next time you watch a game, make up your own scouting report. By concentrating on detail, you will add greatly to your knowledge of the game.

3. Court choice or choice of serve depends on court condition.

4. Substitutions can be a strategic weapon only if you have a strong bench. Often a substitute can add a special talent, such as a tough serve or expert blocking, which will turn the game in your favor.

5. Have a prearranged set of team signals.

15

THE CHANGEABLE
GAME

Any Number: While six on a side is standard for the collegiate, national, and international game for both men and women, just about any number can play volleyball. With more than six on a team, however, the game will always be informal, and it must be said that there are practical limits. Ten players in a 30′×30′ court is a crowd. It still can be fun, but this kind of play will not really improve your teamwork.

With numbers under six, however, you certainly will improve your game, and small-team volleyball, particularly doubles and the four-on-a-side game, have become very popular. These games can be highly competitive, and they lend themselves well to tournament play that delights both participants and spectators.

Another game that is enjoying growing popularity is volleyball with mixed sexes.

The Coed Game: Coed or mixed-sex teams can be composed of two to six players. The major challenge in coed play is a special rule on ball touching sequence. If the ball is touched more than once in your court, for instance, one of the touches must be made by a woman. Also, serving order and positions must alternate—a man and then a woman. On odd-numbered teams, two players of the same sex will serve consecutively, but this is not allowed on even-numbered teams.

Net height is the regulation eight feet for coed play. This means that the women on the team usually have difficulty blocking and spiking, and strategy must be adjusted accordingly. Otherwise, coed teams can play the same aggressive game that all-men or all-women teams play. Indeed, with the caliber of competitive play, particularly on defense, shown by many of the young women players today, the popularity of coed volleyball is bound to continue growing.

Doubles: Rules are generally the same for doubles as they are for six on a side. Usually, substitutions are not allowed, however, and games are sometimes played to eleven rather than fifteen points. When played indoors, the court is often shortened by five feet on each side.

This forces pinpoint serving and spiking, and you may have to sacrifice some power for accuracy.

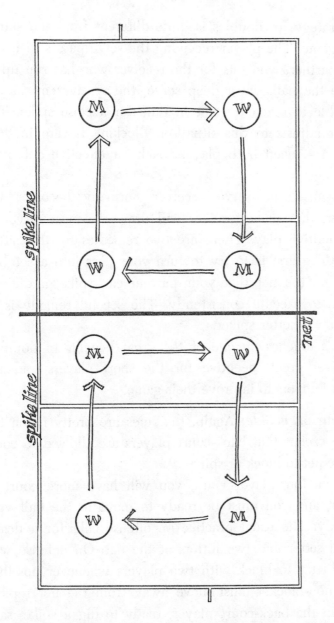

Alternate, man-woman alignment for four on a side, coed volley-ball, showing the clockwise lines of rotation that assure a switch of sex each time the serve is changed.

Strategy for doubles is quite different from the standard game. The player receiving the serve passes to his or her partner, who sets for the receiver who has run up to spike the ball. On a deep serve, the receiver might not be able to reach the net in time for a close spike. The setter adjusts to this situation. Blocking is rare in doubles. You need both players back for effective defensive coverage.

Because the serve receiver normally becomes the spiker, the weakest spiker will draw the most serves in competitive play. There are two remedies for this situation. The first is to try to turn your pass into a set ball close to the net that your partner can spike, a difficult tactic to execute consistently. The second remedy is to become a better spiker.

This touches on one of the great benefits of doubles. It gives great incentive for the short players and the weak jumpers to improve their game.

Four on a Side: Again, the rules are pretty much the same except that back-court players are allowed to come to the net to block or spike.

On a four-player team, you will have more court to cover, and you must be ready to move to the ball very quickly. The usual practice on offense calls for a designated setter and two hitters at the net. On defense, you should try to block with two players whenever possible. The non-blocker must move away from the net rapidly to join the back-court player, ready to dig a spike, save a ball deflected off the blockers, or pass a dink shot.

Four-player volleyball, sometimes played as a necessity when a full squad does not report for practice, will sharpen your court sense and teach you to move far and fast. It forces you to begin anticipating plays, and that will help you in any game.

The Beach Game: Playing on sand changes the game substantially. Sand gives underfoot. That means you must put more muscle into all your moves, including your jump.

Although the net is lowered to seven feet, nine inches for soft sand and seven feet, ten inches for hard sand, you will still have a hard time at first getting up high enough for effective blocking and spiking. Playing in sand, however, does strengthen muscles, and it has another advantage. You can make rolls and dives on the soft sand that you would never attempt on a hard court. Defense can be a spectacular phase of the beach game.

Wind and sun are additional factors that must be considered. This is why teams change sides every five points, equalizing any one-sided advantages. Other rule differences allow a player to step across the center line as long as he or she does not interfere with an opponent.

Coed play is popular on sand, and you will see doubles, three-on-a-side, and four-on-a-side games, but by far the most popular beach game is doubles. It has some special rules.

The service line is not restricted to the back third of the right-hand third of the base line. Instead, the server may stand any place behind the base line. Blockers may not reach over the net, and the two time outs allowed run for a full minute instead of thirty seconds each.

In any kind of outdoor game, the hardest adjustment for beginners is often the wind, particularly on the serve. With the wind behind you, a hard serve can easily carry out, and it will take extra muscle and good spin to place an into-the-wind serve accurately. The receiver will have just as much, perhaps more, trouble than the server in handling the effects of the wind. A ball can die suddenly or veer at the last minute, forcing a desperation pass. It takes experience to use the wind to advantage on serve and avoid surprises on serve reception.

Tips

1. The game in any form will help you improve your volleyball skills.
2. Don't make the mistake of thinking a coed game or beach play cannot be serious. Give your best effort whenever you participate in a competitive game.
3. Although there are minor rule changes for the variations on the standard game, strategy must be changed substantially. Doubles is vastly different from six-on-a-side volleyball.
4. The beach game will build both muscles and skills. Many of this country's top international stars come from Southern California, the capital of beach volleyball.

Though born in Los Angeles, RICHARD B. LYTTLE is really a product of rural California. He graduated from high school in Ojai, served in the Navy in the 1940s and attended the University of California at Berkeley, where he majored in English and professed boxing as his sport. He graduated with a B.A. degree and several bruises. Mr. Lyttle worked as a cowboy, farmer, newspaper reporter, editor, bartender, and school bus driver. He began selling stories and articles for children in the 1950s. He sold more than 150 articles before turning to books.

The author has retained an interest in sports, particularly sailing, tennis, track and field, bicycling, and baseball. He is an enthusiastic camper and trout fisherman.

Mr. Lyttle, his wife, Jean, and their children live in a small town north of San Francisco and next door to the Point Reyes National Seashore.